Card Games

&

Tricks

by Elin McCoy

*With a bonus section on Dice Games
by Joe Gannon*

Mud Puddle Books
NEW YORK

FOR GAVIN

Card Games & Tricks
by Elin McCoy

ISBN: 978-1-60311-233-8

Originally published as
Cards For Kids:
Games, Tricks & Amazing Facts
© 1991 by Elin McCoy

Dice Games by Joe Gannon

Interior design and illustrations by Michelle Gengaro

Special contents of this edition
© 2010 by Mud Puddle Books

Mud Puddle Books, Inc.
54 W. 21st Street
Suite 601
New York, NY 10010
info@mudpuddlebooks.com

Printed in China

CONTENTS

INTRODUCTION

When I was about five years old, I learned to play cards at my family's summer cottage in Michigan. My cousins and I whiled away hours on rainy days playing Go Fish, War, Concentration, Poker, and lots of other card games. We usually played in the boathouse surrounded by fishing gear, sails, oars, paddles, and who knows what else. My mom loved solitaire games, so we learned those, too. Now my son is doing the same thing with his cousins! That's why I wrote this book.

The nice thing about cards is that there are so many different things you can do with them, even in a small place like an airplane seat or car. You can play simple or complicated card games, ones that take a long time to play or only ten minutes, and games just for one person or a whole group. You can make up your own card games and change the rules when you feel like it. You can spend hours building a house from cards or entertain your friends with foolproof card tricks.

The first part of this book is all about the things you need to know before you play: how to count cards; what a suit is; how to shuffle, cut, deal, and score. If you already know how to play some card games, skip most of this part. But be sure to take a look at the section on card manners just to remind yourself how to be a good sport. When you have time, take a look at the amazing facts about cards and stories of famous card players. Also, because there are lots of special terms in card playing, a card glossary is included; so if you see a term you don't understand, here's where to look it up.

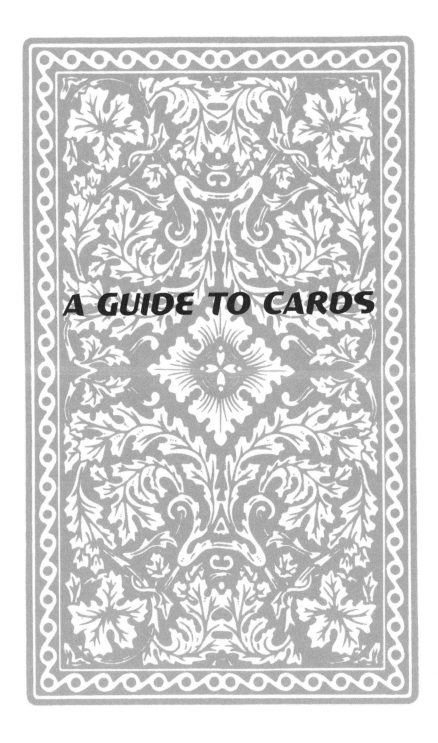

A GUIDE TO CARDS

COUNTING CARDS

The first thing you need to know is that a deck of cards is a set of cards, usually fifty-two, that have numbers and pictures on them.

The number cards, which are also called *spot* cards, have a number in two corners and *spots* or *pips* in the center. These will either be hearts, diamond shapes, cloverlike shapes called *clubs*, or little spearhead shapes called *spades*. The number of spots on the card matches the numeral on it, like this:

The number cards are: ace, which usually counts as one, 2, 3, 4, 5, 6, 7, 8, 9, and 10.

When you are counting points, which you do in some games, remember that number cards have the same value as the number on them. A 3 is worth 3 points. A 10 is worth 10 points. That's called the *face value*.

The odd card in all this is the ace. In some games an ace is worth 1 point, but often it's worth 11 points. Sometimes it can be both. How did the ace get its name? The word comes from the Latin word *as* (pronounced ace), which means a unit or one.

Cards are also called *high* or *low*. A 3 is a low card, 5 is higher, and a 10 is usually the highest of the number cards. The ace can be the lowest (when it equals 1) or the highest (when it equals 11). Game directions always tell you whether the ace is high or low.

CARD ROYALTY

The picture cards, which are also called *face* cards or *court* cards, have a picture of royalty on them. The Jack has the letter *J* in two corners, the Queen has a *Q* in two corners, and the King has a *K* in two corners, like this:

All these cards are worth more than a number card, but they don't have any special number value. The Jack is the lowest face card, then comes the Queen, and the King is the highest. But in games where the ace is high, it is higher than the King.

Court or royalty cards, showing Kings and Queens, were in the earliest decks of cards in Europe; the American kind of card deck came from Europe.

Have you noticed the crazy clothes the King, Queen, and Jack wear? These costumes are based on what real kings and queens in England wore in the 1500s.

There haven't been many changes in the court cards since.

THE STORY OF THE JOKER

There are lots of other strange things about the cards we use. One of the strangest is the two extra cards that come with every deck, the jokers. Sometimes the joker is pictured as a jester dressed in colorful medieval clothes complete with cap and bells, like this one:

But sometimes jokers have other pictures or designs, like horses.

Even though card decks always come with jokers, most card games don't use them. They are only used in card games as wild cards. (A wild card can be whatever number or suit a player wishes.) Jokers are also useful if you lose one card in a deck –you can just write that number on the joker card.

How did the joker get into card decks? It's an American invention. It became part of the regular deck during the 1860s in the United States because of a game called *euchre*. This popular game needed a deck with an extra card that was higher than all the others, so manufacturers put a blank card called the *euchre* card in each deck. Supposedly, the word *euchre* was misspelled by people and eventually became the word *joker*.

THE TRUTH ABOUT ONE-EYED JACKS

If you look at the four Jacks in a deck of cards, you'll notice that two of them are in profile, with only one eye showing. These are called the one-eyed Jacks. In poker games, players sometimes make these Jacks wild cards. Lots of people think these one-eyed Jacks must have had some special meaning in the past, but they didn't. In early card decks Kings, Queens, Jacks, and other figures were shown many different ways: standing, on horseback, with a full face showing, in profile, and so on. It just happened that the early card decks made in Rouen, France, had one-eyed Jacks in their decks. These were the decks that most printers in England copied, and the English deck is the one that came to America.

WHAT'S A SUIT?

Card decks are divided into four suits of thirteen cards each. Look at the cards in your deck. Do you see a special design on the face of each one? Those are the symbols for the four suits. They are sometimes called *spots* or *pips*. Two suits are red: hearts ♥ and diamonds ♦. Two suits are black: clubs ♣ and spades ♣. The thirteen cards in each suit go from ace to King or two to ace.

Suits have been part of card playing for centuries. One set of early Korean cards had seven suits. Early Islamic decks used four suits, the way we do, but the Islamic suits were coins, cups, swords, and polo sticks. Some experts think they represented people serving the sultan. The oldest European decks used four suits, too, which stood for the four parts of medieval life. Cups represented the church; coins, the merchants; swords, the nobles and soldiers; and batons, the peasants and farmers. (These symbols are still used on cards in Spain and Italy.) In Germany hearts, acorns, leaves, and bells were used. Around 500 years ago, card makers in France invented the suit signs we use today.

AMAZING FACTS ABOUT CARDS
& FAMOUS CARDPLAYERS

♥ No one knows who invented the first card games. Historians and card experts think cards were invented in China, over 1,000 years ago.

♠ Playing cards first came from Europe to the Americas with sailors on Columbus's voyage in 1492.

♦ There weren't any numbers on cards in the first European decks. Players had to count the number of suit symbols on each one.

♣ Cards have been made in all shapes and sizes—square, oblong, even round.

♥ Early cards in America were made from leaves and from the skin of sheep and deer. Some card decks at the beginning of the 20th century were even made from aluminum.

♠ The earliest cards in Europe were very, very expensive because each deck had to be made and painted by hand. Ordinary people couldn't even afford to buy cards until the printing press was invented in the 1400s. Printing cards was as important to printers as printing books.

♦ Playing card companies have secret recipes for the paper and coatings used in making cards. The paper is laminated and coated with china clay, titanium dioxide, castor oil, and other ingredients so you can't see through it; then it's run through a crusher, which smooths it before the cards are printed, varnished, and cut apart.

♣ Card playing was illegal in the Puritan colonies of seventeenth-century New England. Adults paid a fine if they were caught once. The second time they could be whipped in public—even if they just had a pack of cards in their house.

♥ George Washington loved to play cards. He recorded in his diary just how much he won and lost at cards each week.

♠ Thomas Jefferson played cards to relax while he was writing the Declaration of Independence.

♦ Benjamin Franklin printed and sold cards and used them in some of his electrical experiments.

♣ Playing cards were once taxed everywhere. That's how the strange design on the ace of spades started in England in 1628. So people couldn't avoid paying a tax on each deck of cards, the government passed a law requiring card printers to have a special design for the ace of spades and to purchase a tax stamp to put on the design before the deck could be sold. The tax lasted for almost 350 years.

♥ Wild Bill Hickok was shot in the back during a poker game in the Nuttal and Mann Saloon in Deadwood, South Dakota, in 1876. Even today poker players call the card combination Hickok was holding—a pair of aces and a pair of 8s—a "Dead Man's Hand."

♠ Women were hot card players in western boom towns. One, Doña Gertrudes de Barceló of Santa Fe, won enough money at Three Card Monty to buy supplies for the American Army during the 1848 Mexican War.

- ♦ Annie Oakley, the best sharpshooter in the West, used the ace of hearts in one of her most important tricks. She pinned it on a tree twenty-five yards away, then fired twenty-five shots in twenty-seven seconds to shoot away the heart in the center.

- ♣ During the Civil War, card decks were changed to be more patriotic. Some had Union generals instead of Kings; others had American flags and stars for the red suits and the shield and American eagles for the black ones; still another had infantry officers for Kings, goddesses of liberty for Queens, and artillery officers for Jacks.

- ♥ The biggest poker game in American gambling history was probably the one that took place in 1900 at the Waldorf-Astoria Hotel in New York City. The people playing were a famous poker player named John (Bet-a-Million) Gates and some of his friends. That game involved a million dollars.

- ♠ The longest card game ever played is probably a bridge game played by four students at Edinburgh University in Scotland in 1972. It lasted 180 hours! That's according to the Guinness Book of World Records.

- ♦ The most popular card games in America today are Bridge, Poker, and Gin Rummy.

- ♣ More than 100 million decks of cards are sold in the United States every year.

- ♥ The most money ever paid for a deck of cards was over $100,000. The Metropolitan Museum of Art in New York City paid that in 1983 for a deck of Flemish cards made in the fifteenth century.

HOW TO SHUFFLE AND WHY

Before you start a game, you want the cards to be completely mixed so that suits and numbers aren't in any special order. (Otherwise one person might get all the high cards or a lot of pairs, and that wouldn't be fair.) Mixing the deck is called *shuffling*. You should shuffle the cards twice before each game.

There are easy and hard ways to shuffle. Start with the easiest.

SUPER EASY SHUFFLE

If you're playing with little kids, this is the shuffle to teach them.

Spread all the cards face down on the floor. Push them around to change their places. Pick them up in random order.

That's it!

OVERHAND SHUFFLE

This is the next easiest shuffle. Gather all the cards into one pile. Hold them in your left hand. With your right hand, lift small batches of cards from the back or middle of the deck and put them in front of the deck. You can also lift batches from the front of the deck and put them at the back.

THE RIFFLE SHUFFLE

Kids younger than six have difficulty with this shuffle, mostly because their hands are too small. When you're learning how to do it, look carefully at the pictures below. Usually it's easier to understand how to do this shuffle from pictures than to read about it.

Gather the cards into one pile, then divide it into two piles that are about equal. Place them so that the short ends are next to one another, like this:

Hold one pile in each hand. Your thumb should be at one end, your little, ring, and middle fingers at the other, and your index finger curled to rest on top of the pile, like this:

Bend the cards up at one end with your thumbs. Let go of one card from one pile, then one from the other pile by lifting up your thumbs. The cards should drop gently so they overlap one another. Keep letting go of one card at a time until they all overlap, like this:

Slide them together into a single pile, like this:

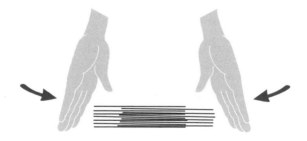

Then hold the deck and tap one long side against the table to straighten the cards.

Don't be discouraged if it takes you a while to learn how to shuffle this way.

Just keep practicing!

HOW TO CUT CARDS AND WHY

Cutting the cards after they're shuffled helps prevent cheating. It's an extra way to mix the cards in case the players have seen the bottom card while the deck is being shuffled, or if the dealer arranged them in a special way so a particular player would get good cards. You don't *have* to cut the cards. But most people do.

After the dealer shuffles the deck twice, he straightens and squares it face down on the table. The player to his left is the one who cuts the deck. The player lifts up the top part of the deck, puts it down on the table, and then puts the bottom part on top of it.

That's all there is to it!

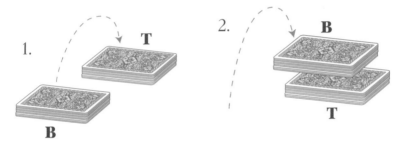

HOW TO DEAL AND WHO GOES FIRST

Before you can play a game, you have to hand out cards. That's called *dealing*. The dealer is the person you choose to hand out the cards. Usually the dealer is the person who shuffles the cards, too.

CHOOSING A DEALER

There are lots of fair ways to choose a dealer. Here are two: (1) Spread the cards face down on the table and have every player pick a card. Whoever has the highest card is the dealer. Say in advance whether ace is high or low. (2) Take turns drawing cards from a face-down deck until someone draws an ace. Then that person is the first dealer.

Usually a person is only a dealer for one game. Then the player on his left becomes the next dealer. Sometimes the person who wins the game is the next dealer.

HOW TO DEAL

Hold the deck of cards face down, keeping your hand across the bottom card. (You don't want anyone to see it.) Give the top card to the player on your left. Give the next card to the player on her left. Keep dealing to the left across the table, ending with the dealer. Then start a new round. Always deal one card at a time unless the game directions say to deal more. Try not to let players see the faces of the cards as you deal.

WHO GOES FIRST

The player to the left of the dealer is almost always the first one to play her cards.

CARD MANNERS

Card manners don't have anything to do with the actual rules of the game. They are concerned with the way players usually handle the cards, treat one another, and what they do about mistakes. This list will give you some ideas, but find out how *your* friends want to play. Some kids like to collect the cards and deal all over again no matter what the mistake.

1. Agree on the rules of the game ahead of time. For example, how you'll score; what you have to do to win; and what you'll do about mistakes. Then play by the rules.
2. Deal all cards face down (unless the rules for a game say to deal them face up). If a card lands face up by mistake, bury it in the deck so no one knows where it is. Deal a new card to that player.

3. Wait until everyone gets their cards before you touch or pick up yours.
4. Don't peek at anyone's cards.
5. Hold your cards so that no one can see them. Don't hold them far out or down so that other players can't help seeing them.
6. Wait your turn to play during the game.
7. Here's how to act when you win: Don't brag about it. That just makes everyone feel jealous.
8. Here's how to act when you lose: Don't argue. A good loser is someone who is cheerful and generous to those who win. It's good sportsmanship to congratulate another player—"You sure had a great hand," or "You sure were lucky. Maybe I'll win next time." Remember that a card game is just a game. If you're losing a lot, suggest playing a different game.
9. Be a good sport. That means playing the best you can—without cheating—and not getting mad when you lose. It means recognizing that no one can win all the time.

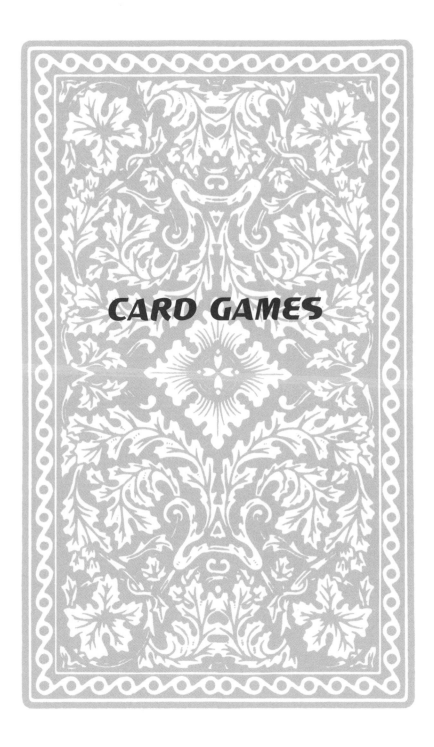

CARD GAMES

PIG

This very silly game is more fun when a whole bunch of kids play. The most important thing is to keep your eyes on the other players so you won't end up being the Pig.

DEALING

From a regular deck (fifty-two cards) remove one set of four of the same number or picture for each player. It doesn't matter which sets you take out. If you have five players, you need twenty cards–four each. (How many will you have for ten players?) With thirteen kids you'll use the whole deck.

Shuffle the sets of cards together and cut. Then deal four cards to each player, one at a time.

HOW TO PLAY

Arrange the cards in your hand so that matching cards are together. When the dealer says, "Go," all players quickly pick one card they don't want and put it face down to their left.

Then everyone picks up the face-down card to their right. If it matches a card in their hand they put it next to that card.

As soon as the dealer says, "Go," again, everyone chooses another card to pass to the left. Players keep passing and picking up cards trying to be the first to get four matching cards.

When you get four of a kind, you stop passing cards and put a finger on your nose. Everyone else must stop passing, too, and

Strategy hint:
You're trying to get four cards that match. So if you have a pair, put down one of your other cards.

quickly put their fingers on their noses. The last one to do so is the PIG. Whoever loses five times is the prize PIG and has to shout, "Oink! Oink!"

P.S. In this game, it's okay to tell the player next to you to hurry up and pass.

CONCENTRATION

NOTE: NUMBER OF PLAYERS 2 TO 6

Don't start playing this game unless you can really pay attention to what's going on! The person with the best memory will be the winner. And guess what? Often the youngest player wins. The point is to use your memory to help you collect the most pairs.

DEALING

Shuffle and cut the cards. Spread all the cards face down on a table so they don't overlap. You can arrange them in face-down rows instead.

Hint 1: The game is easier when you arrange the cards in rows.

Hint 2: When playing with younger children (under six), use only twenty-six cards (half a deck), making sure there is one pair of each rank (Kings, 2s, 6s, etc.).

HOW TO PLAY

The dealer starts. He turns any two cards face up, one at a time. If they make a pair (like two 10s or two aces), he puts them face down in front of himself and then turns over two more cards. A player keeps his turn as long as he turns over pairs. If the cards don't match, he turns them face down again exactly where he found them. Now it's the next player's turn.

You can guess the strategy to win. If you play close attention to the cards that are turned back down again, you'll be able to remember where a lot of different cards are. Then when you turn up a King, you'll remember where its match is.

When all the cards have been picked up, the player with the most cards wins.

GO FISH

NOTE: NUMBER OF PLAYERS 2 TO 5

Play this regular version of Go Fish with kids who are at least six years old. The object is to collect the most sets of four matching cards, like four Jacks or four 3s.

DEALING

Shuffle and cut the cards. Deal five cards, one at a time, to each player. Put the rest of the cards face down in a pile in the center of the table.

HOW TO PLAY

Arrange your hand so that matching numbers or pictures are together. If you have four of a kind–that's called a *book*–put them face up in front of you.

The dealer goes first. When it's your turn, you ask any player for cards that match one you have. Suppose you have two 8s, two 6s, and one King. You say, "Katharine, do you have any 8s?" Katharine has two, so she must give you both of them. You put down the four 8s and ask Justin for 6s. He doesn't have any and says, "Go fish." You must draw a card from the center pile. If it is a 6, you take another turn. If it isn't, the turn passes to the player on your left, and so on around the table.

Guess what! The player on your left is Katharine. She has one 6. Since she heard you ask for a 6, she knows you have at least one. When she asks you, you have to give her both your 6s. That's an example of how the game works.

Players can keep asking or fishing as long as they get the card they asked for.

When a player gets a book, he always puts them face up in a pile in front of himself.

The player who has the most books wins the game.

WAR

War is one of the easiest games to learn and play, but don't let that fool you! It's also very exciting, fast, and lots of fun. The whole point is to win all the cards.

DEALING

Shuffle and cut the cards. Deal one card at a time to each player until all the cards are gone. Depending on how many kids play, a few players may get an extra card. That's okay.

HOW TO PLAY

Each player puts her pile of cards face down in front of herself. Then everyone turns the top card in their piles face up. Whoever has the highest card wins all the face-up cards and puts them at the bottom of her pile. (Ace is the highest in this game.) Then everyone turns over the top cards again, and so on.

So far, so good. This game gets exciting when war starts.

Here's how it happens: Two kids turn over cards that are alike. They might be two Jacks or two 10s or two 8s. The two kids have a war to see who will win all the face-up cards.

Here's what they do: Each kid takes the top card from her pile and puts it face down without looking at it. Then each player takes another card and puts it face up. Whoever has the higher face-up card wins the war, and takes all the face-up and the two face-down cards.

Keep playing until someone wins all the cards. That player is the winner.

P.S. If more than two kids are playing, the two cards that are alike have to be the highest cards played in that round to start a war. Only the two kids with matching cards are in that round of war.

OLD MAID

NOTE: NUMBER OF PLAYERS 3 OR MORE

This is an old, old game. You can use a regular deck of cards or you can use one of the special Old Maid decks sold at book, stationery, and variety stores. These contain matching pairs of characters–usually very funny ones–and one card with a picture of the "Old Maid." You could even make your own Old Maid deck.

Whichever you use, the point of the game is the same: to match all the cards in your hand, to make pairs, and not get stuck holding the "Old Maid."

DEALING

Take out all the Queens except the Queen of clubs if you are using a regular deck of cards. That will be the "Old Maid." Then shuffle and cut the cards. Deal out all the cards, one at a time. It doesn't matter if some kids have an extra one.

HOW TO PLAY

Check to see if you have any pairs. Put all your pairs face down in front of you. Then arrange the rest of your cards in a fan.

The dealer starts. When it's your turn, pull a card from the hand of the player on your left. No peeking! If you get a card that matches one in your hand, you show the pair and put it down with your other pairs. If the card doesn't make a pair, you just keep it in your hand. Don't show it to anyone. Then the player on your left turns to his left neighbor and picks a card and so on around the table.

When all the cards are paired, one person will be left with the Queen of clubs. That person loses the game.

Strategy hint: If you have the Queen of clubs during the game, you want to get rid of it. That means someone else has to pick it out of your hand. Some kids carefully arrange their cards so that the Old Maid sticks up. Usually this strategy does not work. A better trick is to fake out other players by having a different card stick out. Most kids will go for the *least* obvious card.

SUIT OF ARMOR

NOTE: NUMBER OF PLAYERS 3 TO 5

This is a very easy game to learn and play. You want to be the first player to have all the cards in your hand belong to the same suit–clubs, hearts, spades, or diamonds.

DEALING

Shuffle and cut the cards. Deal one card at a time to each player until everyone has seven cards. Put the rest of the cards in the center of the table.

HOW TO PLAY

Look at your hand! See which suit you have the most of. If you have three clubs, a heart, two spades, and a diamond, for example, you'll want to try collecting clubs. But don't tell anyone which suit you're trying to collect!

The dealer starts. He puts one card of a suit that he doesn't want face down. Then the player on his left puts down a card he doesn't want, and picks up the card the dealer put down. Then the next player to the left puts down an unwanted card, and picks up the second player's discard. The play around the table goes on this way until one player has all seven cards of the same suit and cries, "Suit of Armor."

P.S. You may change the suit you want to collect as the game goes on.

BEGGAR-YOUR-NEIGHBOR

NOTE: NUMBER OF PLAYERS ONLY 2.

This is a fast, exciting game that depends strictly on luck. The point? To capture all the cards.

DEALING

Shuffle and cut the cards. Give each player twenty-six cards.

HOW TO PLAY

Hold your stack of cards face down in front of you. The person who didn't deal starts. He turns the top card of his stack face up, and puts it in the center of the table. The dealer does the same thing, putting his card on top of the first card. You both take turns turning over cards until one of you turns over an ace, King, Queen, or Jack. That's when the game really gets going.

Here's how. When player 1 turns over an ace or picture card, player 2 has to put extra cards from the top of his stack face up in the center pile as a penalty. He puts out four cards for an ace, three for a King, two for a Queen, and one for a Jack. If all the penalty cards are numbered 10 or under, the first player gets to take the whole center pile, including the penalty cards. He puts the pile face down underneath his stack of cards and puts out his top card to begin a new center pile. But if one of player 2's penalty cards is a picture card or an ace, everything is reversed. Then player 1 has to pay a penalty, and player 2 captures the cards.

The more who play, the sillier the game will be.

Eventually one player will capture all the cards. This can take a short or long time. Whoever gets all the cards is the winner.

What makes this exciting is that you don't know who will win until the very last minute.

DONKEY

NOTE: NUMBER OF PLAYERS 4 TO 13

Here's a fun variation on the game of Pig. The point in this game is to avoid being the DONKEY by snatching one of the buttons in the center of the table when the time comes.

DEALING

You need one set of four matching cards (numbers or pictures) for each player. If six kids are playing, for example, you'll need six sets of four matching cards, or twenty-four cards. You'll also need some buttons. Put one *less* button than there are players in the center of the table. For six players, you'll need five buttons.

Shuffle the sets of cards together and cut. Deal one at a time to each player until they're all gone.

HOW TO PLAY

When the dealer says, "Go!" pass a card face down to the person on your left and pick up the card passed to you from your right. Keep passing and picking up cards as quickly as possible, checking to see if you have four matching cards. Eventually someone will end up with four of a kind in her hand. Then she can grab a button; she must try to do it without anyone noticing. Everyone else grabs a button as soon as they notice her doing it.

One kid won't get a button. That player has the letter *D* (for donkey) marked down against her.

Shuffle, deal, and play again. If the same person doesn't get a button again, she now gets an *O* next to her *D*. Or perhaps someone else will get a *D* marked against her. The game is over when one player gets all six letters: *D-O-N-K-E-Y*. She is the donkey and must bray "Hee-haw!" as she runs around the other players.

P.S. Check after button grabbing to make sure that the winner *does* have four of a kind. If not, she's the donkey right away.

SPIT

In this game, you have to be alert as well as fast! The record time for a game between kids who were real experts was only two minutes.

This isn't a game to play with your little brother or sister. It's the most fun with someone who is just about as good as you are.

DEALING

Shuffle and cut the cards. Divide the deck into two equal piles. Each player gets one pile called his *stock*.

HOW TO PLAY

Hold your stock in one hand, face down. Both of you put four cards from your stock face up in front of you. That's called your *spread*. The whole idea is to be the first to use up your stock and spread.

Now you're ready to start. You play at the same time: Count together, one . . . two . . . three . . . SPIT. On the word SPIT you each slap the top card of your stock face up between the two spreads, starting two center piles. You get rid of your spread cards by putting them on top of your center pile or your opponent's center pile. BUT you can only put a card on a center pile if its rank is one above or one below the top card on the pile. If one pile has a 3 on it, you can put a 2 or 4 on top of the 3. If you put a 4 down, you can put a 3 or a 5 on that, and so on. Play your spread cards as quickly as possible. When there's an empty place in your spread, fill it with a new card from your stock.

When neither of you has a spread card that you can put on a center pile, stop for a break, then say, One . . . two . . . three . . . SPIT again, slap the top card from your stack on your center pile, and keep going until one player has no more cards in his stock or spread. Whoever is out of cards takes the smaller center pile to be his new stock. The other player takes the larger one.

Shuffle your stock and start again. Keep playing until one of you is completely out of cards. That's the winner.

P.S. One important rule: You can only use *one hand* (the hand not holding your stock) to put cards on the center pile.

CRAZY EIGHTS

NOTE: NUMBER OF PLAYERS 2 TO 4

Card historians think Crazy Eights was invented over 200 years ago in England, and that it was first called *Comet* after the comet predicted by Edmund Halley. Now the game is sometimes called *Eights,* and sometimes *Crazy Jacks*. But the point of all of them is the same: to be the first player to get rid of all his cards with the help of a *wild* card.

DEALING

Shuffle and cut the cards. With two players, deal seven cards to each. With more players, deal five cards to each. Put the rest of the cards face down in a pile in the center of the table. This is called the *draw pile*.

Turn over the top card in the draw pile to start a pile of face-up cards next to it. This is the *discard pile*. If the turned over card is an 8, bury it in the middle of the draw pile and turn over another card.

HOW TO PLAY

Start with the player on the dealer's left. Everyone takes turns putting a card from their hand face up on the discard pile. That sounds easy. But it has to match the number, picture, or suit of the top card in the pile, or it can be an 8. In Crazy Eights, any 8 is a wild card. That means you can change its suit to whatever you want it to be.

Here's an example of how the game works. If there is a 4 of hearts on top of the discard pile you have to put down another 4 of any suit, any card with hearts on it, or any 8. If you put down a 4 of clubs, the

Strategy hint: You can play an 8 whenever you want to, but it's best to use them only:
1. When you have to.
2. When you have a lot of cards of one suit that you want to get rid of.
3. When another player has only one or two cards left. You want to make sure you don't have it in your hand when a player runs out of cards. If you do, he or she will get 50 points!

next player has to put down another 4, any card with clubs, or an 8. If you put down an 8 you can change its suit to whatever you wish. Then the next player will have to put down another 8 or a card with the suit you've chosen.

If you don't have a card with the right number or suit or an 8, you keep drawing from the draw pile until you get one you can put down.

P.S. If the draw pile is gone, you have no card you can put down, and the game hasn't ended, you have to pass.

The game ends when one player is out of cards; that player is the winner. It also ends if no one can play any more cards, and the draw pile is all gone. Then the player with the fewest cards wins.

The winner collects points from the cards left in everyone else's hands.

Here's how to score:

• Eights	50 points each
• Kings, Queens, Jacks	10 points each
• Aces	1 point each
• Number cards	The number of points is the same as the number on the card. A 4 equals 4 points.

Set up a goal. The first player to reach 200 points, for example, can be the winner.

HEARTS

This game used to be called *Reverse*. Why? Because the point of the game is to get the *least* points by not winning any hearts. Watch out!

DEALING

Shuffle and cut the cards. Deal one at a time to each player until they are all gone. All players should have thirteen cards.

HOW TO PLAY:

Organize your hand so that all cards of each suit–clubs, spades, hearts, diamonds–are in order from low to high. Two is low; ace is high.

Choose three cards from your hand that you don't want. Pass them face down to the player on your left. Then pick up the cards that have been passed to you and organize your hand again.

The person on the dealer's left starts. If that's you, put any one of your cards face up in the middle of the table. This is called the *lead card.*

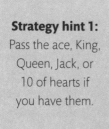

Strategy hint 1: Pass the ace, King, Queen, Jack, or 10 of hearts if you have them.

The player on your left puts a card of the same suit on top of the lead card. Then the player on her left goes, and so on. Whoever plays the highest card in that round takes the trick. That means she takes all four cards and puts them in a stack in front of her.

The player who takes the first trick leads the next round by putting out any card she wishes.

If you don't have a card of the same suit as the lead card, you can put any card you wish on top of the stack. It can't win the trick no matter how high it is.

Keep leading and taking tricks until everyone is out of cards. Then you count the number of hearts in the tricks you've won. Each heart counts one point. The player with the least hearts is the winner.

Strategy hint 2: You don't want to win tricks that contain hearts. So put out low cards when you have to lead. Save your high cards to play when you can see that there are no hearts in the trick. Play hearts when you don't have any cards with the suit of the lead card.

CASINO

NOTE: NUMBER OF PLAYERS 2 OR 3

Both kids and adults who tried out the games in this book found this was one of the most exciting ones. It's a good choice when you want to play a game with your parents. You may find yourself hooked on it, too! But pay attention to all the steps in the directions because Casino is complicated to explain, even though it's not that hard to play. In fact, kids can often beat grown-ups!

DEALING

Shuffle and cut the cards. Deal two cards at a time until each player has four. Put another four cards face up in the center of the table. Set aside the remaining pack of cards. When the players use up the four cards in their hands, deal another set of four to each and so on throughout the game. When the four face-up cards are gone, deal out four more throughout the game.

HOW TO PLAY

The player on the dealer's left starts.

When it's your turn, you want to take a face-up card from the middle of the table by matching it with one in your hand if you can. That's called *taking a trick*. There are three ways you can do it.

1. You have a card in your hand that matches a face-up card. Put yours on top of the matching card and take both as a trick. If you have a 5 and there is a 5 on the table, for example, you can take it. If there are two 5s on the table you can take both on one turn. (You can't take two picture cards–King, Queen, or Jack–on one turn.)

2. You have a card with a number that is equal to the numbers on two or more face-up cards added together. You can take all on one turn. For example: a four and a two are among the face-up cards. You have a 6 in your hand, so you can take both. Ace equals one. If three or four face-up cards add up to a number in your hand, you can take all of them in one trick.

3. You can *build* a trick on one turn and take it on the next. Suppose you have a 2 and 7 in your hand and there is a 5 among the face-up cards. On one turn you put the 2 on top of the 5 and announce, "Building 7." On your next turn you take the two cards with your 7.

P.S. You can only build a number you have in your hand. And you must take your build on your next turn.

38

But beware! There is a danger in building. Another player who also has a 7 may take the two cards before your next turn! Or someone who has a 9 may pick up the built-up 7 and a 2 on the table because 2 + 2 +5 = 9. Or someone may build on top of your build. He could put down an ace on top of the 5 and 2, announcing, "Building 8."

You won't always be able to take a trick or build. If you can't, you must put one of the cards in your hand face up with the others.

The game ends when all the cards have been dealt and no one has any cards left. The player who took the last trick gets any extra face-up cards on the table.

Now it's time to add up everyone's score. Check with this table to figure out how many points you have.

The player with	Points
The MOST cards	gets 3
The MOST spades	gets 1
The Big Casino (10 of diamonds)	gets 2
The Little Casino (2 of spades)	gets 1
An ace (each ace counts one point)	gets 1

The player with the most points is the winner.

BLACKJACK

NOTE: NUMBER OF PLAYERS 3 TO 10

This fast-moving game was invented in France, where it is called *Vingt-et-Un* (vant-ay-unh), which means twenty-one. There's one very unusual thing about this game–each person plays against the dealer. You win if you get Blackjack–cards that add up to 21 points–or if your cards add up to a number closer to 21 than the dealer's cards. But if you go over 21 points, you go *bust* and are out. This game is a little complicated to play, so plan on a few practice rounds before you really get going. Winning doesn't just depend on luck.

DEALING

Pick someone to be the first dealer. When someone gets Blackjack he becomes the next dealer.

Strategy hint: The basic rule is to ask for another card if you have 13 points of less. If you have 17 points or more you should stick. With 14, 15, and 16 points, check the dealer's face-up card before deciding. If it's an ace, picture card, or 10, play safe and stick.

P.S. The traditional way to pick a dealer in Blackjack is by giving a face-up card to each player until someone gets an ace.

Shuffle and cut the cards. Most people bet buttons or chips when they play this game, but you don't have to. If you do, give each player at least thirty chips or buttons. Put extra chips in the center of the table. That's called the *kitty*. You put all your bets down before you get any cards.

Give everyone one card face down. Then go around again, dealing each player a face-up card.

HOW TO PLAY

Everyone looks at their cards and silently adds up their point to see if they have Blackjack–exactly 21 points. Picture cards are worth 10 points, aces can be 1 or 11, and number cards are worth the number shown on them. If the dealer has a Blackjack, he shows his cards. He wins and that hand is over. If you're playing for chips, he collects everyone's bet from them. Any other player with a Blackjack collects only the dealer's bet from him. If both the dealer and a player get Blackjack, the dealer and player split everyone else's bets.

However, if just one player or no players have Blackjack, the game isn't over. Then the dealer asks one player at a time, "Do you stick?" In Blackjack language that means: "Do you want to keep just the cards you have, or do you want another one to see if you can get your total card points closer to 21?" You can get as many more cards as you want.

Sometimes it's hard to decide if you want more cards because you don't want to risk getting more than 21 points and going bust. Check the strategy hint for help.

A player who says, "Hit me," gets another face-up card from the dealer. He can keep saying "hit me," and getting cards until he says, "I stick," or goes bust. Anyone who goes bust says, "I fold." He turns his cards over, and gives the dealer his chips. A player's turn ends when he sticks or busts.

Then the dealer asks the next player to his left, "Do you stick?" and so on around the table. The dealer has the last turn.

Everyone who didn't go bust turns over their cards. If the dealer goes over 21, he pays everyone still in the game the amount he bet. If the dealer's cards are closest to 21, the other players pay him the amount they bet. The dealer pays his bet to any player who is closer to 21 than he is.

Collect the cards and put them face up at the bottom of the deck. The dealer doesn't reshuffle until he reaches a face-up card.

RUMMY

There are lots of rummy games. This is the basic one. Once you've played it, you'll find all the variations easy to understand. Rummy is a good game to play with grown-ups because they usually don't get bored.

DEALING

Shuffle and cut the cards. Deal them face down, one at a time. The amount of cards each player gets depends on the number of kids playing. For two players, give ten cards each. For three or four, give seven, and for five or six, give six.

Put the rest of the cards in a pile, face down. That's called the *stock*. Turn over the top card to make a discard pile next to it.

HOW TO PLAY

In this game you try to get rid of your cards by grouping them together in *melds* and then laying the melds face up. A *meld* is a set of three or four of a kind, like three 4s or four Kings, or a sequence–called a *run*–of three or more cards of the same suit, like the 7, 8 , 9, and 10 of clubs. In this game, ace is only low, so you can have a sequence of: ace, 2, 3, 4, but *not* Queen, King, ace.

Take a moment to put your matching cards and runs together before you start.

The player on the left of the dealer starts. Turns go to the left.

Take the top cad from the stock or discard pile. If you have any melds, lay them face up like this:

Then put a card you don't want in the discard pile. And then it's the next kid's turn.

If you can put all your cards down in melds on one turn, that's *going rummy*. Then the game is over and you are the winner.

As the game continues, you may draw a card that fits in a meld you've already put down or in one someone else has put down. You can add that card to the meld when it's your turn. For example, if you or another player have a run of 2, 3, and 4 of clubs, whoever has the 5 or ace of clubs can put them into that meld.

Strategy hint 1: Keep your eyes on the discard pile so you know whether you can get the cards you need for the melds you're trying to make. You might have to try for a different one. If you know which cards other kids pick up from the discard pile, you'll know which melds they're trying to get.

Strategy hint 2: Discard higher cards (like picture cards) that aren't matched early in the game. That way, if you lose, you won't give away so many points.

You keep taking turns around the table until someone is out of cards. That person wins.

HOW TO SCORE

Everyone puts their remaining cards face up. The winner gets points for all the cards left in everyone else's hands. Here's what cards are worth:

- Aces = 1 point each
- Picture cards = 10 points each
- Number cards = the number on the card

Add up the winner's points, then shuffle, cut, and deal again. The first person to get 100 points is the Grand Rummy Champion. But you don't have to play for points. You can make the first person to win five games the champion.

QUEEN CITY RUMMY

This game is like basic Rummy except for three things. Scoring is different, everyone gets seven cards no matter how many players there are, and you must put down all your cards in melds on one turn. That means you have to wait until you have two complete melds in your hand before laying them down. The suspense is that someone else may do it first. Whoever lays down the melds first calls out "Rummy." That's the winner. She gets points for every card laid down. The other players get no points at all.

GIN RUMMY

NOTE: NUMBER OF PLAYERS 2

This is the best rummy game for two players. It's like basic Rummy–you're trying to lay down the same kinds of melds–but there are some very important differences. A lot of kids think Gin Rummy is more exciting.

DEALING

Deal ten cards to each player. Put the rest of the cards face down in a pile (that's the *stock*) and turn over the top card to start a discard pile next to it. That card is called the *up card.*

HOW TO PLAY

Just as in basic Rummy you're trying to get all the cards in your hand to be part of a meld of three or more of a kind or three or more of a sequence in the same suit. But in Gin Rummy you lay down your melds and any extra cards only when you're ready to end the game in a showdown!

The person who didn't deal starts. Suppose that's you. You may take the upcard if you choose. But if you don't want it because it doesn't fit with any of the cards in your hand, you have to let the dealer have a chance to take it. If neither you nor the dealer want it, you draw the top card from the stock. Then you discard a card from your hand that you don't want. Then it's the dealer's turn to draw and discard. You keep drawing and discarding until one player knocks or says, "Gin."

If you don't have any unmatched cards–called *deadwood*–in your hand, you can "Go Gin." On your turn, you draw a card, lay down all your melds, discard a card face down, and call out "Gin." You win. The other player has to lay down all his cards, arranged in melds, with the deadwood on the side. The winner gets 25 points for going Gin. He also gets all the points from the other player's deadwood.

Here's what cards are worth:

- Picture cards   = 10 points each
- Aces   = 1 point each
- Number cards   = the number shown on the card

But you don't' have to wait to lay down your melds until you have exactly two melds and no extra cards. That's why Gin Rummy is full of suspense.

You can ask the other player for a showdown by "knocking" when you have 10 points or less of deadwood in your hand.

Here's how to knock: On your turn you draw a card, lay down your melds, put your dead-wood to one side, discard one card face down, and knock the table once. You're taking a big chance because you don't know

Strategy hint 1: Knocking is risky. You want your deadwood to be worth as few points as possible, so save a few low cards as you play. Discard picture cards early on unless you have a pair. If you can't get a third picture in five or six turns, discard both.

Strategy hint 2: Knock as soon as you can when your deadwood is low cards. Often the other player knocks before you can "go Gin."

Strategy hint 3: Keep your eye on the discard pile.

what the other player has in his hand.

Your opponent has to lay out his melds and deadwood when you knock. But he has one big advantage–he can try to get rid of his deadwood on your (the knocker's) melds. That means he can put an extra Queen, for example, on your meld of three Queens, or put a 6 of spades on your sequence of 3, 4, and 5 of spades. That also means that he can reduce his points of deadwood.

HOW TO SCORE

You both add up your points in deadwood. If the knocker has the smaller number of points, he subtracts his score from the other player's. His score is the difference between the two. But if the other player has a smaller number, he gets the difference *plus* a bonus of 25 points. Why? Because the knocker was the one who wanted a showdown and he lost.

The winner deals the next game.

Keep playing until someone has 100 points.

P.S. The other player can't try to get rid of his deadwood when someone has "gone Gin."

HINTS ON DOING CARD TRICKS

1. Standard card decks come in two sizes. A bridge deck is a little narrower than a poker deck. It's easier to do card tricks with a bridge deck.
2. Practice handling cards. Shuffle them in different ways, turn them over, hold them in your hand, cut them, deal them. The more you do these things the more natural you will look handling cards when you are trying to fool the audience.
3. When you shuffle in a trick, keep the cards as close to the table as possible.
4. Practice your tricks at least twenty times before performing them.
5. Practice doing tricks in front of a large mirror so you'll see what you do, just the way the audience sees you. This is a good way to catch mistakes.
6. Develop a *patter*. That's what magicians call the kind of talking they use while they are doing a trick. You want people to pay attention to what you're saying. You don't want them to notice that you're trying to fool them by turning over a card deck or peeking at a card.
7. Your program should have no more than five tricks. It should last about eight to ten minutes.
8. During your performance, stay relaxed. Go slowly. Most important, combine natural movements with secret moves. Suppose you need to see the bottom card on the deck of cards you're holding. Glance at it when you are shuffling the cards, or when picking them up, or squaring or straightening the deck. All these are ways you can casually look at the bottom card without the audience getting suspicious. The more natural

Strategy hint: Practice glancing at the bottom card so you don't do it in an obvious way.

you can make it look, the more the audience will be fooled. The first few times you try to look natural you will probably end up looking awkward. But just keep practicing.

9. While you're performing, you'll want to add suspense. Pause. Concentrate by putting your hand on your head and closing your eyes. Mumble magic words or rhymes you've made up. Pretend to be puzzled and then say, "Aha!"

ON THE EDGE CARD STUNT

Here's a quick and easy stunt to get your card act started. Ask for several volunteers from the audience. Challenge them to balance a card on its edge in five seconds. They won't be able to.

But you will! Hold the card in the palm of your hand, curving it slightly. Set it down on the table while it is still curved. It will remain curved long enough for you to balance it!

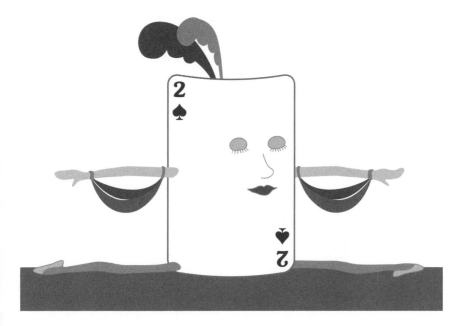

THE DIME-IN-THE-GLASS CARD STUNT

You'll need a heavy glass (not plastic) that is not too wide, a dime, and one card for this stunt. Place the card on top of the glass with the dime in the middle, like this:

Challenge a volunteer to get the dime into the glass without picking up or holding the card or knocking over the glass.

When they can't do it, show them how.

Flick your finger against the edge of the card. It will fly off and the coin will drop into the glass.

FIND THE CARD

You can learn how to do this simple trick in a few minutes. All it takes is a secret glance at the bottom card of the deck for you to identify any card your audience picks from the whole deck.

Here's what to do:

1. Ask for a volunteer from the audience to shuffle the cards so no one thinks you've fixed the deck in a special way.

2. Fan out the cards and hold them so they face the volunteer. Ask him to pick any card, remove it from the deck, memorize it, and show it to the rest of the audience; he must not let you see it.

3. While he is doing this, you slide the cards into a pile, tapping the edges of the cards against the table to straighten them. Slyly sneak a look at the bottom card. Remember the number or picture and suit.

4. Put the deck face down on the table. Ask your volunteer to put his card on top and then cut the cards several times. That way he'll think his card is completely hidden in the deck.

5. Announce that you will now identify the card. Here's the secret. When your volunteer cut the cards, the bottom card ended up on top of his card. The bottom card you memorized will be right on top of that card.

6. Start turning over the cards one at a time. Use your magician's patter and add suspense. Tap the top card of the deck and tell the audience that you're using your magic touch to identify the correct card. Go very slowly.

7. When you turn over the card that you memorized, stop and tap the next face-down card. "Aha!" you can announce, "This will be your card. I feel the magic vibrations." That will be the card your volunteer picked.

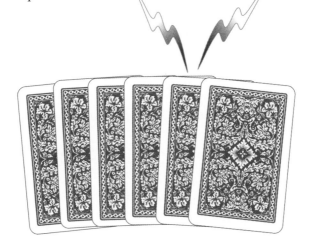

THE X-RAY EYE TRICK

Be warned. Your audience may ask you to do this trick again and again as they try to figure out your secret.

First, ask a volunteer to count out three piles of cards in a special way while your back is turned. He must follow the directions exactly or the trick won't work.

He holds the deck in one hand and turns the first card face up on the table. He starts counting with the number on that card, putting face-up cards on top of it until he reaches the number thirteen.

Here's how: If the card is an 8, he'll count the card he puts face up on top of it as 9, the card after that 10, then the one after that 11, then 12, then 13. After the volunteer reaches 13, he turns the card in that pile face down and starts a new one.

In this trick ace is one, Jack is 11, Queen is 12, and King is 13. So if he turns up a Queen as the first card in a pile, he'll count that as 12 and put down only one face-up card on top of it to reach 13.

The volunteer counts out three piles of cards, turning each one face down as he finishes it. He puts the remaining cards in a pile to the side.

You turn around, count the number of cards in the pile of remaining cards, then ask the volunteer to turn face up the top card on any two piles.

You're going to use your X-ray vision to identify the top card on the third pile.

Concentrate hard. To get the answer you have to do some secret arithmetic in your head. First you need the number of leftover cards.

In this case it's thirty-one. Then you need to add the two face-up cards together. Here the cards are Jack and 5, so the sun is sixteen. Then add 10 to the sum (you always add 10, no matter what the face-up cards are). That makes twenty-six. Now you subtract that number from the number of leftover cards. So in this example, you'd subtract twenty-six from thirty-one. The answer you get will be the number of the top card in the third pile. Here, it's 5.

Your answer will always be right!

P.S. Make sure your deck has fifty-two cards. If it doesn't, the trick won't work.

THREE-COLUMN CARD MAGIC

This foolproof trick depends on the way you pick up the cards. If you do it right, you'll have no problem finding any card chosen by someone in your audience:

HOW IT WORKS

1. Ask for a volunteer from the audience to shuffle the cards. Then deal a row of three face-up cards, going from left to right. Next deal an overlapping row below it, then another, and another, until there are seven face-up cards in each column, like this:

2. Ask the volunteer to visually pick a card and tell you which column it is in. Remind her not to tell you which card it is, to stare at it, or give you any other clues.

3. Slide the cards in each column together to make a pile. Don't change the order of the cards in each column.

4. For the trick to work, you must pick up the three piles in a special order. Put the pile that has the volunteer's card in it *between* the other piles.

5. Turn the cards face down and deal three columns again, just as you did before. Then ask your volunteer which column her card is in this time. (It's usually, but not always, in a different column.)

6. Pick up the cards again, making sure you keep the order of the cards in each column and that you put the column with the volunteer's card between the other two.

7. Deal again, just as before, and have the volunteer point to the column in which her card appears now. Pick up the cards in the correct order again.

8. Turn the cards face down. Use a little magician's patter. Say a few magic words over the cards or wave a magic wand over the card pile.

9. Turn over the cards slowly, one at a time, counting silently. Pause after you've turned over the tenth card. Close your eyes, then predict that the next card will be the chosen card. The eleventh card will always be the volunteer's card.

THE SECRET DEAL

In this trick you're going to identify two cards chosen by someone in the audience. And you'll be able to do it just by the way you deal the cards.

Follow each step exactly:

1. Give the deck of cards to someone in the audience. Ask him to shuffle them and deal six face-down piles of five cards each.

2. Now ask him to choose and memorize two cards from the remaining deck without letting you see them. He can show them to the audience, but not to you.

3. Have him put the two cards face down on any two of the six piles. Make sure you notice and remember which piles he puts the cards on, but don't let anyone know that it is important to you.

4. You have to pick up the piles in a special order for the trick to work. Casually pick up one of the piles with an extra card first. Then slide two regular piles on top of it. Now put the other pile with the extra card on top, and then put the last two regular piles on top of that.

5. Deal all the cards into two piles, starting with one card on the left, then one on the right, then one on the left again, one on the right, and so on.

6. When all the cards are in two piles, ask your volunteer to choose one of the two piles. You'll adjust what you say according to which one he picks, because you'll need to deal from the pile on your left. So if he points to the pile on the left, say, "We'll use the left pile for the rest of the trick." But if he picks the pile on the right, announce, "You'll have the right pile and I'll take the left one."

7. Deal the left pile into two piles, starting with one card on the left, one on the right, another on the left, another on the right, and so on.

8. When you're finished, pick up the new pile on the left and start dealing another two piles, one to the left and one to the right again, just as you did before.

9. Once again, pick up the pile on the left. It should have four cards in it. Deal two piles again, starting with the left, then the right, then the left, then right.

10. Pick up the pile on the left, turn over the cards, and announce, "These are your cards." They will be.

NEEDLE IN THE HAYSTACK

This trick takes careful preparation and some good magician's patter so your audience won't catch on to the secret. Once again you're going to identify a card chosen by someone in the audience.

Here's how it goes:

Step 1. Before your performance, fix the deck so that all the red suit cards are in one pile and all the black ones are in the other.

Step 2. At the performance, hold one of the two piles face down in a fan, like this:

Put the other pile face down on the table where you can reach it easily. Ask for a volunteer from the audience to pick a card from the fanned cards you are holding.

Step 3. Tell her to write down what the card is without showing it to you or telling you what it is.

Step 4. Now for the tricky part. While she is concentrating on writing, you casually switch the two piles of cards, putting down the one you are holding and picking up the other pile.

Step 5. Then turn your back to your volunteer and hold that pile of cards behind your back. Ask her to put her card back into the pile that you are holding. Point out that you can't see the card she has picked.

Step 6. Turn around again and shuffle the pile of cards you're holding, keeping them close to the table. Look through the cards without letting anyone see them and pick out the volunteer's card.

Can you guess how you'll do it? If the pack has red suit cards, her card will be the black one. If the pack has black cards, her card will be the red one.

P.S. Hold the pile carefully so your volunteer can't see that all the cards are red or black.

THE AMAZING BLINDFOLDED CARD READER

Here's another easy trick to master. It will be very mysterious to your audience how you can tell which card a volunteer picked. Why? Because you'll be blindfolded. The key to the trick is to be able to add and subtract.

You'll need a pencil and paper as well as a blindfold and a deck of cards.

Step 1. Remove the ace, 2, 3, 4, 5, 6, 7, 8, and 9 of spades from your deck. Ask a volunteer to blindfold you. Then hand her the nine spades, the paper and the pencil.

Step 2. Ask the volunteer to pick any five cards (out of the nine cards) and add up their value. An ace counts as a 1. She should discard the other four cards.

Here's a sample:

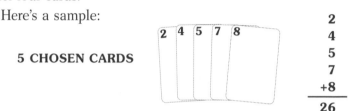

5 CHOSEN CARDS

```
  2
  4
  5
  7
 +8
────
 26
```

Step 3. Have the volunteer pick one of the five cards. She can hide it in a pocket or give it to a friend to hold.

Step 4. Now ask your volunteer to put the four cards that are left in a row like this:

4 REMAINING CARDS

She must write down the four-digit number they make. (7842)

Step 5. Have your volunteer subtract the number she wrote down in Step 2 from the number she wrote down in Step 4 and tell you her answer. (7842 - 26 = 7816)

Step 6. Now it's time to identify the hidden card. Use some magician's patter while you're doing the arithmetic that will help you figure out what the hidden card is.

You add all the digits in her answer together. The sample answer here is 7816. You would first add

$$
\begin{array}{r}
7 \\
8 \\
1 \\
+6 \\
\hline
22
\end{array}
$$

and get 22.

Step 7. Then you add the two digits in that answer together. In this sample, you would add 2 + 2 and get 4.

Step 8. Last, you subtract that answer from nine. For example, you would subtract four from nine. Your answer is the number of the hidden card! In this case it's five.

P.S. 1. If you get nine as the answer in Step 7, that is the number of the hidden card.

P.S. 2. Build suspense in this trick by tapping your forehead, muttering magic words or phrases, and wiggling your fingers in the air to catch the *vibrations* from the card.

THE SPELLING TRICK

This is a good show-off trick that little kids love to watch and that even six-year-olds can do. You're going to turn up the cards whose name or number you spell. It just takes a little preparation.

Here's what you do:
1. Remove the ace, 2, 3, 4, 5, 6, 7, 8, 9, 10, Jack, Queen, and King of one suit from your deck.
2. Arrange those cards face up in this exact order: 3 first, 8 (on top of the three), 7 (on top of the eight), Ace, Queen, 6, 4, 2, Jack, King, 10, 9, then 5.

3. Turn over the pile of cards. Now they are all face down.
4. Tell your audience that you will turn over the card whose name you spell, starting with the ace.
5. Holding the cards in one hand, put the top card at the bottom of the pack, and say, "*A*." Do the same for the next card, saying the letter, "*C*." Say, "*E*" as you put the third card at the bottom of the pile. Then say, "Here comes the Ace," and turn the fourth card face up. Put the ace on the table and continue.
6. Spell the next, *T-W-O,* in the same way, by putting one card at the bottom of the pack each time you say a letter. Then turn over the fourth card, and put it face up on the ace. Say, "Here comes the two." Leave the 2 on top of the ace and continue.
7. Do the same thing for 3, 4, 5, 6, 7, 8, 9, 10, Jack, and Queen.

Even when you only have a few cards, you put the top card at the bottom of the cards each time you say a letter. The last card will be the King.

THE INCREDIBLE FREE-FORM CARD TOWER

Do you have patience and determination? You'll need both plus a lot of practice to build this tower of cards.

This is the way Jackson built his. It was the design that worked the very best.

WHAT TO DO

Hold the long edges of each card between your thumb and first, middle, and ring fingertips, like this:

Lean the top short edges of two cards against one another to make a tent, like this:

Lean cards against the two open ends, like this:

Then learn cards around the sides. This will make the bottom of your tower very stable. Make two more tents the same way, right next to the first tent. Your base should look like this:

Strategy hint 1: Work with a friend. That way you won't get so frustrated. When the cards fall down for the tenth time, just laugh.
Strategy hint 2: Build your tower on a flat rug, not a completely smooth surface. If you want to build on a table, spread out a tablecloth or placemat or even a sheet of paper toweling and build on top of that.

Now make a floor. Hold a cards so it faces the table and drop it *gently* on top of the tower base. Drop several cards so that they overlap until you have a solid floor, like this:

Strategy hint 3. A used, worn deck of cards works best.

Build tents on top of the floor the way you built the base. Go slowly. Don't scream if the tower falls over!

Keep building floors and tents on top of them. Make your tower as high as you can. Believe it or not, some nine-year-olds have built a tower with five levels.

CARD GLOSSARY

black card A card with clubs or spades. In some solitaire games you put any black card on any red card.

cut To lift off the top part of a face-down deck. Put the top on the table, and then put the bottom part of the deck on top. The player on the dealer's left cuts the cards after they have been shuffled.

deal Handing out the cards to the players from the deck. You deal the top card first, usually to the person on the dealer's left.

dealer The person who shuffles the cards and hands them out.

deck A regular set of fifty-two cards.

deuce A card with the number 2 on it.

discard To put down a card you don't want at the end of your turn. Usually you put it in a discard pile, right next to the rest of the deck.

draw To take the top card from the rest of the deck after the cards have been dealt.

face card A King, Queen, or Jack.

face down This means the picture or number side of the card does not show.

face up This means you can see the picture or number side of the card.

fan To hold your cards so you can see the corner of each one, like this:

four of a kind Four cards that match in number or picture but not suit, like four Queens, or four 10s.

follow suit To put down a card of the same suit as the card just played.

foundation card   A card you build up or down on in solitaire games. This card is usually an ace or King.

hand   The cards you are holding in your hand during a game.

lead   To play the first card. Usually the player to the left of the dealer leads.

meld   A set of three or more cards with the same number or picture, or a sequence of three or more cards of the same suit, which is placed face up on the table. In all Rummy games this is how you win.

pack   A deck.

pair   Any two cards that match by number or picture, like two 3s or two Kings.

picture card   A King, Queen, or Jack.

red card   A card with hearts or diamonds on it. In some solitaire games you can put any red card on a black card.

round   This means each person in the game has had a turn to play a card.

shuffle   To mix up the cards so that the same suits and numbers aren't together. You always shuffle the cards before you start a game.

spot card   Any card with a number on it or an ace.

spot value   The value of the number on the card. The spot value of a 3 is 3 points.

stock   The cards that are left over after dealing.

suit   One of four special designs that appear on the cards. They are hearts, spades, clubs, and diamonds.

tableau   The pattern in which you lay out cards in solitaire.

trick   When each player puts one face-up card in the center of the table on one round of play, the pile of cards is called a *trick*. The highest card wins the trick. In some games, such as Casino, you take a trick when you can match a face-up card on the table with one from your hand.

trump   A number or suit you've picked to be extra powerful in a game, such as Hearts. Those cards will then be higher in value than any other cards.

wild card   A card that can be whatever number or suit you want it to be. In the card game Crazy Eights, 8s are wild. In most games, jokers are wild.

DICE GAMES

Dice have been used in games and gambling since ancient times—they were popular with the early Egyptians, Greeks, and Romans, and there is evidence of their use from the far flung regions of Eastern Asia to the ruins of prehistoric British fortresses, and from the Germanic tribes of Northern Europe to the earliest civilizations of Africa and the Middle East. The oldest known dice are part of a 5000-year-old backgammon set discovered by archeologists in southeastern Iran. Early dice were often made from the ankle bones of hoofed animals, and "bones" has long been used as a slang term for dice—in fact, the Arab word for knuckle bones is the same word they use for dice today. Later dice were made from ivory, stone, clay, wood and metal, and today's dice are almost all made of plastic.

Dice can have many different configurations of sides and markings but the common dice used in most games are small cubes with slightly rounded corners, usually about ½ to ¾ inch (1.3 to 1.9 cm) along an edge, and marked on each side with patterns of dots representing the numbers 1 to 6. Opposite faces of a die (the singular of dice) will add up to seven—thus, six is backed by one, five by two, and four by three.

The dots marking each side of a die are called "pips." On high quality casino dice, the pips are created by drilling small indentations into the surface of the die and then filling them with a contrasting color of paint that exactly matches the density of the material from which the die is made, so that each die remains perfectly smooth and balanced. That balance allows the dice to produce a truly random result when thrown. Though some dice games use only one die, most use between two and five, and casino dice are commonly sold in packs of five. Dice should be thrown onto a flat surface, either directly from the hand or from a "dice cup," a container that allows the dice to tumble freely ensuring a random result.

ACES IN THE POT

Any number of players can join in this game making it ideal for large groups of friends or family. This game is full of second chances that can make for exciting comebacks.

Requires: At least two players, two dice, and two counters per player. *Counters can be poker chips, buttons, coins, marbles, etc.*

1. Give each player two counters.
2. To determine who will take the first turn, each player rolls a single die once. The player who rolls the highest number goes first in the game.
3. On your turn, roll both dice:

   a) If an ace (a 1) is thrown, put a counter in the middle of the table (the pot).

   b) If two aces are thrown, put two counters in the pot.

   c) If a 6 is thrown, give a counter to the player on your left.

   d) If two 6s are thrown, give that player two counters.

   e) If an ace and a 6 are thrown put one counter in the pot and give one to the player on your left.

4. After you roll, play passes to the player on your left.
5. As play continues, only players who still have counters can roll the dice, but players who have no counters remaining should stay in the game since they can receive counters from other players who roll 6s.
6. The last player to have any counters left must roll the dice three times without rolling a 6 in order to win the round.
7. If a 6 is rolled, one counter is passed to the left and the game

> **Hint:** This game can be frustrating and difficult for very young players who may often overlook combinations that could be used. If youngsters are playing with adults it can be a good idea to let the adults help them find the usable combinations in a roll.

continues until one of the players is again the only one with any counters remaining. That player must then make three rolls of the dice without throwing a 6 in order to win.

8. In the following round play begins with the player to the left of the player who started the previous round.

BEETLE

Great for younger players or for parents and their children. Beetle is a simple game that is visual and easy to follow.

Requires: At least two players (*ideal for four to six, for more it is best to divide into teams*), 1 die, pen or pencil and paper for each player.

1. Give each player a sheet of paper and a pen or pencil.
2. To determine who will take the first turn, each player rolls a single die once. The player who rolls the highest number goes first in the game. Or, if you choose, let the youngest player go first.
3. The goal is to be the first to complete the drawing of your beetle. Each beetle must be made of thirteen parts: the body, the head, two eyes, two antennae, six legs, and a tail. The body must be drawn first, and the head must be drawn before the eyes or antennae are added.
4. On your turn you roll the die and the number you roll determines what body part you may draw. To draw the body you must roll a 1, then a 2 for the head, a 3 for each leg, a 4 for each eye, a 5 for each antenna, and a 6 for the tail.
5. You must roll a 1 before you can draw anything since the body must be drawn first. The head, legs, and tail may be added any time after the body is drawn, but the eyes and antennae can be

added only after the head is drawn.

6. The first player (or team) to complete the beetle wins the round.

7. In the following round play begins with the player to the left of the player who started the previous round.

Variation: To speed play you may decide that the roll of 3 allows you to add three legs to your beetle.

OHIO

Also called Centennial or Martinetti, this is a racing game that requires the players to do a bit of simple calculation as they speed around the board.

Requires: At least two players (*up to eight can play*), three dice, a dice cup, a board consisting of 12 boxes numbered 1 to 12 (*easily drawn on a sheet of paper*), and one marker for each player (*markers can be poker chips, buttons, coins, marbles, etc.*).

1. Give each player a marker.

2. To determine who will take the first turn, each player rolls a single die once. The player who rolls the highest number goes first in the game.

3. The object of the game is to move your marker up through all of the boxes from 1 to 12 and then back down again from 12 to one.

4. On your turn, roll all three dice. One of them must come up 1 to place your marker in box 1. You then need to roll a 2 to move to box 2. You must move through each box in order, but you can use any value or combination of values on the dice to make your moves. So, if you are lucky enough to roll a 1 and a 2 on your first

roll, you would move through box 1 to box 2 on that roll. In fact, perhaps the luckiest roll in the game is to roll a 1-2-3 combination on the first roll, in which case you can move not only to box 1, box 2, and box 3, but also on to box 4 (3+1), box 5 (3+2) and box 6 (3+2+1).

5. It is not necessary to use all of the numbers that come up on the dice, so long as some value or combination of values from the throw matches your next sequential destination box.

6. If you have moved your marker on a roll, you get to roll again. If you cannot move your marker, the turn passes to the player on your left.

7. Be careful to try all of the possible combinations of the dice results to see if there are any you can use. For instance, when you are trying to roll an 11 you might roll a 6-5-6. If you're not careful, you might only move to box 11 (6+5) and not notice that you can also move to box 12 (6+6).

8. If you could have used a combination and overlook it, that number can be "claimed" and used by any other player who needs it as soon as you roll again or pass the dice. The first one to claim it gets it.

9. The winner is the first player to race up through every box to 12 and then back down to box 1.

CRAPS

This is the most famous dice game of all and is played in gambling casinos throughout the world. It developed in the 12th century from an old English game called Hazard. The modern casino game is played on special a table and includes a large number of complicated bets that are placed on the table's specially marked surface. Though you could purchase a craps table or board for home, a simpler private-play version of craps betting is described here.

Requires: At least two players, two dice, a flat surface on which to roll the dice, and counters for each player to use in placing their bets (*counters can be poker chips, buttons, coins, marbles, etc.*).

1. Before the game is begun, all of the players should agree on a maximum bet.
2. The person rolling the dice is referred to as the "shooter." The first shooter places a bet, let's say ten counters, in the middle of the game area, and states the amount of the bet, "I'll shoot ten."
3. The shooter is betting that he will win. The other players have the option to "fade" his bet— that is, to bet *against* his winning. The shooter's bet must be "covered" by the other players. For example, one other player might place a ten-counter fade bet, or five other players may each place two-counter fade bets. As you see, the total of the fade bets must equal the shooter's bet. If not enough fade bets are made to cover the shooter, the shooter withdraws some of the original bet so that it matches the fade betting.
4. The shooter wins immediately if he rolls a 7 or an 11, and loses immediately if he rolls a 2, 3, or 12. If any other number is rolled, it becomes the "point" and the shooter will continue to roll the dice.
5. On subsequent rolls the shooter is trying to roll the point again. If the shooter rolls a 7 before the point is rolled the shooter loses and the dice are passed to the player on the left. If the shooter makes the point before a 7 is rolled the shooter wins the bet(s) and has the option to continue to roll the dice or to pass the dice to the next player.
6. If the first roll establishes a point, there are a number of "side bets" that other players may place among themselves. A "come"

bet is a bet that the shooter will make the point before throwing a 7. This bet will be placed against another player's "don't come" bet (that the shooter will not make the point). Come and don't come bets are not even odds bets because the odds of making a point vary depending on what number the point is. Such bets should be made as follows: if the point is 6 or 8 the bet is made at 6 to 5 odds against making the point, if 5 or 9 is the point the odds are 3 to 2, and if the point is 4 or 10 the odds are 2 to 1.

7. Another common side bet is the "hardway" bet. Similar to the come bet, a player who places a hardway bet is hoping that the shooter will not only make the point but also that it will be made the hardway—that is, with doubles. So, if the point is 4 the shooter must make the point by rolling two 2s for the hardway bettor to win. Since it is less likely that the point will be made the hardway, the odds are higher on this bet. If the point is 6 or 8 the bet is made at 10 to 1 odds against making the point, and if the point is 4 or 10 the odds are 8 to 1.

Strategy: It is useful to know that there is a very slight advantage to betting against the shooter with a "fade" bet—over the long run only 49.3% of the possible outcomes are winners while 50.7% are losers. Of course, casinos add a "bar double-six" rule so that if the shooter looses with a double-six, your fade bet (called a "Don't Pass" bet in casino Craps) does not win. That shifts the odds in favor of the casino. Remember, the odds in casino gambling *always* favor the casino.

DROP DEAD

This is a fast moving game that works well for a large number of players.

Requires: At least two players, five dice, a dice cup, and a pencil and paper to keep score.

1. To determine who will take the first turn, each player rolls a single die once. The player who rolls the highest number goes first in the game.
2. On your turn, roll all five dice. If any dice come up 2 or 5 those dice are now "dead" and the roll will not count toward your score. Remove the dead dice that came up 2 or 5 and roll again.
3. If, on any roll, no 2s or 5s come up add up the values of all dice thrown on that roll and add it to your score.
4. Then roll the remaining dice again following the same rules: if any come up 2 or 5 they are dead, no score, take them out and roll again, but if no 2 or 5 appears add the total to your score.
5. When all five dice are dead, that player whose turn it is has "dropped dead" and the dice pass to the player on the left.
6. Once all of the players have taken their turns the highest scorer is the winner.

Variation: Each player rolls the dice once and counts up the total of points showing other than 2s or 5s. Record both the points and the number of dice the player has left after removing the dice that came up 2 or 5. Pass the dice around the circle of players each rolling in turn and recording both the points and the dice remaining. Keep taking turns rolling until all of the players have "dropped dead." High score wins.

STRAIGHT SHOOTER

This game is also known as Hearts or Hearts Due, and may be played with special dice that substitute the letters H-E-A-R-T-S for the pips representing 1-2-3-4-5-6. It works just as well with standard dice.

Requires: At least two players, six dice, a dice cup, and a pencil and paper to keep score.

1. To determine who will take the first turn, each player rolls a single die once. The player who rolls the highest number goes first in the game.
2. On your turn, roll all six dice. The goal is to roll straight sequences that start with 1. The longer the straight the higher the score, as shown on this scoring chart:

1 = 5 points
1-2 = 10 points
1-2-3 = 15 points
1-2-3-4 = 20 points
1-2-3-4-5 = 25 points
1-2-3-4-5-6 = 35 points

3. If on any turn three of the dice come up 1s, the player's whole score is erased and the player starts again at zero in the next round.
4. After the roll, record your score and pass the dice to your left.
5. The first player to reach or exceed 100 points is the winner.

Variation: If you want a longer game simply raise the value of the goal to 150 points or even 200.

HELP YOUR NEIGHBOR

This game is called Help Your Neighbor because every throw of the dice has the potential to do just that.

Requires: two to six players (*six is best*), three dice, a dice cup, and ten counters per player. *Counters can be poker chips, buttons, coins, marbles, etc.*

1. To determine who will take the first turn, each player rolls a single die once. The player who rolls the highest number goes first in the game.
2. That player will also be numbered "Player 1." Each of the players is numbered in clockwise sequence, so the player to Player 1's left is Player 2, and so on.
3. If there are only two players assign each of them 3 numbers; for instance Player 1-2-3 and Player 4-5-6. If there are 3 players assign them each 2 numbers. If there are 4, 5, or 6 players assign each a single number and then ignore any unused numbers that come up during the rolls of the dice.
4. On your turn, roll all three dice. For each die that matches your player number (or numbers) put one of your counters in the middle. At the same time, the other players—your *neighbors*—should also put one counter in the middle for each die that matches one of their player numbers.
5. Keep going until one of the players runs out of counters. That player is the winner.

INDIAN DICE

Indian dice is played very similarly to the card game poker, but you use dice instead of cards.

Requires: At least two players, five dice, a dice cup, and a pencil and paper to record the hands.

1. To determine who will take the first turn, each player rolls a single die once. The player who rolls the highest number goes first in the game.
2. On your turn, roll all five dice. Your goal is to make the best "poker" hand from the dice rolled. 6s are high and deuces (2s) are low. Aces (1s) are wild (aces can be used as any other card). The possible hands are ranked as follows:

   a) Five-of-a-kind is the highest hand. (e.g., 6-6-6-6-6 or 2-2-2-2-2)
   b) Then, four-of-a-kind (e.g., 5-5-5-5)
   c) Then, full house (three-of-a kind plus a pair—e.g., 1-1-3-3-3)
   d) Then, three-of-a-kind (e.g., 2-3-4-4-4)
   e) Then, two pairs (e.g., 1-1-5-5-6)
   f) Then, one pair (e.g., 1-2-3-5-5)
   g) Then, highest value 6 (e.g., 1-2-3-4-6)
   h) Then, highest value 5 (e.g., 1-2-3-4-5)

3. If you like the outcome of your first roll, you can "stand pat" and record that as your hand, passing the dice to your left. But just as in draw poker, if you think you can improve your hand by re-rolling some or all of the dice you

are free to do so. You may then stand on that hand or re-roll some or all of the dice one more time. But that's the limit, after the third roll you must accept the hand that is showing.

4. No subsequent player in the round may take more throws than the player who started the round.

5. After everyone has thrown, the highest hand wins the round. In the unlikely event of a tie, the other players drop out and the highest hands play off against each other until there is only one left with a high hand.

6. A game is usually made up of three rounds with the winner taking the best of three.

Variations:

Rather than making the ones (aces) wildcards, simply treat them as the highest value just as an ace would be in a game of cards.

Though it is not customary to allow straights in Indian Dice, you could decide to allow for straights (five consecutive values such as 1-2-3-4-5) in your game. If you choose to, a straight would rank below a full house and above three-of-a-kind.

THIRTY SIX

A very simple fast moving game, great for large groups of players.

Requires: At least two players, one die, a pencil and paper to record the scores, and a supply of ten counters for each player. *Counters can be poker chips, buttons, coins, marbles, etc.*

1. Give each player ten counters.

2. To determine who will take the first turn, each player rolls the die once. The player who rolls the highest number goes first in the game.

3. Each player places one counter in the middle (the pot).
4. On your turn roll the die and record your score on the paper. After each roll keep a running total of your score. If your score goes over 36 you are out of the round.
5. The goal is to have your total come closest to 36 without going over.
6. Once your score is 31 or higher you may choose to pass the dice without rolling, allowing your score to stand. This does not prevent you from rolling in subsequent rounds if you wish.
7. If someone reaches 36 exactly they immediately win the round.
8. If no score totals 36 exactly, play continues until there is only one player left that has not gone over.
9. Once all players have totals of at least 31, players are no longer allowed to pass, they must roll and try to beat the high score. The high score does not have to roll again unless another player has jumped ahead to become the new high score.
10. The winner of the round collects the counters in the pot, and the next round starts with the player to the left of the one that started the first round. The player with the most counters at the end of all the rounds is the winner of the game.

YACHT

Yacht is very similar to General, a popular dice game in Puerto Rico. The commercially available game Yahtzee is based on Yacht.

Requires: At least two players, five dice, a dice cup, and a pencil and paper to record the scores.

1. Make up a score sheet for each player including the player's name and a list of the scoring categories as follows:

Yacht

Big Straight
Little Straight
Four-of-a-Kind
Full House
Choice
6s
5s
4s
3s
2s
1s

To determine who will take the first turn, each player rolls a single die once. The player who rolls the highest number goes first in the game.

2. On your turn, place all five dice in the cup and roll. You may use the values from the first roll, or you may choose to roll some or all of the dice again. If so, pick up the dice you'd like to change and re-roll. Again you may stand with that outcome, or you may re-roll some or all of the dice one final time.

3. Once you have completed your roll, you must select one scoring category to be used in recording your score for this round. Points are assigned according to the following chart:

Yacht (five-of-a-kind) – 50 points
Big Straight (2-3-4-5-6) – 30 points
Little Straight (1-2-3-4-5) – 30 points
Four-of-a-Kind – total pip value of all five dice
Full House (three-of-a-kind plus a pair) – total pip value
Choice (no particular combination of values) – total pip value
6s, 5s, 4s, 3s, 2s, OR 1s – total pip value of only the dice showing the selected number

4. After you have recorded your score, pass the dice to your left for the next player to roll.

5. There are twelve rounds in a game. There are also twelve scoring categories. Each scoring category is to be used only once during the twelve rounds of the game. You must select a scoring category for each round as it is played even if the score that you have earned in that category is 0.

6. When all players have completed twelve rounds the game is over. Total each player's score. The high score is the winner.